be a winner in
HORSEMANSHIP

be a winner in
HORSEMANSHIP

BY CHARLES COOMBS

Illustrated with 43 Photographs and Diagrams
William Morrow and Company
New York 1976

Library of Congress Cataloging in Publication Data

Coombs, Charles Ira (date)
    Be a winner in horsemanship.

    SUMMARY: Discusses the selection and care
of a horse and the fundamentals of horsemanship.
    1. Horsemanship—Juvenile literature.
[1. Horsemanship]   I. Title.
SF309.2.C66   798′.23   76-17118
ISBN 0-688-22080-0
ISBN 0-688-32080-5 lib. bdg.

ACKNOWLEDGMENTS FOR PHOTOGRAPHS
American Quarter Horse Association, page 30; Carnation-Albers, pages
12, 19, 22, 26, 42, 45, 60, 109; Lynn Dixon, pages 76, 115; Pacific
Coast Quarter Horse Racing Association, page 24; United States Depart-
ment of Agriculture, pages 17, 20, 23, 57, 59, 63, 96, 107; Western
Harness Racing, Inc., page 31.
All other photographs were taken by the author.

contents

For Lynn,
a delightful daughter
and a real horsewoman.

foreword

This book has been years in the making. It began when our daughter Lynn was about twelve. Then, as always, she loved horses. "Daddy," she would urge, "please write a book about horses."

Meanwhile, as she grew into a fine young woman, she began raising and training quarter horses. Wild Chablis, her prize-winning mare, is the gray horse seen in many of the photographs in the book, and Lynn is the girl most often pictured. After all, would I have dared illustrate it in any other way?

The book is a matter of pride to both of us. Lynn was an integral part of it from the early discussions and chapter outlines to the final polishings. She also shot a few of the photographs. Without her help throughout, the task would have been infinitely more difficult.

But there was, in addition, help from eager and enthusiastic "horse people." Both individuals and companies provided research materials, illustrations, and counsel. The book began to take shape and make sense during the period that I hung around corrals and attended horse shows armed with notebook and camera.

There was valuable, willing cooperation from many young horsemen and horsewomen, who displayed their skills before the camera and explained the reasons for what they did. Among them were Haila Hitt, Roger and Val Silverstone, my veterinarian-son Dan, and farrier Sam Morano.

I hope this book is worthy of our combined efforts and a worthwhile pleasure for you to read as well.

Charles "Chick" Coombs
Westlake Village, California, 1976

chapter one
HORSE AND RIDER

The friendly and skillful teamwork between a horse and its rider can be a most exciting and rewarding partnership. The partnership, however, is not achieved casually. Horsemanship, the art of riding and caring for horses, develops only after long, patient work between an eager rider and a noble mount.

How or where you make your first contacts with riding horses is not important. Many young horsemen and horsewomen begin by renting a mount from a local stable. Even an hour on the back of some dusty steed that is bent upon getting back to the stable can serve as a starting point in learning the lessons of horsemanship. And most reputable stables pride themselves in having decently trained and fairly sprightly horses for hire. Summer camps, dude ranches, a vacation trip, a visit to the country are other typical instances and places where you may come in contact with horses. But you cannot honestly call yourself a horseman or horsewoman until you have spent the time and effort necessary to become at least a fairly accomplished rider. You also must learn to understand horses and to take care of them.

There are numerous reasons for wanting to ride and be around horses. Perhaps it is the companionship with one of the earth's most beautiful, graceful, and intelligent creatures. Possibly it is the satisfaction a ninety-pound boy or girl gets out of being able to control a twelve-hundred-pound animal. Sometimes it is the motion, rhythm, and balance in horsemanship that appeals to equestrians. In addition, there are the sights, sounds,

Companionship with a horse is a rewarding adventure.

and smells of the sport, which have their own familiar and special attraction. Certainly there is the challenge of discipline, which works both ways between horse and rider, with neither completely dominating the other.

Your willingness to accept responsibility is a major factor in mastering horsemanship. There is nothing easy about training or caring for a horse. Learning to ride properly is not the simple matter of climbing aboard a horse and putting your heels to its flanks. Horsemanship calls for daily work and responsibility that takes much of your free time. Happily, the rewards usually make up for the sacrifice.

For most young people, interest in riding horses begins with fantasy. You may imagine you are John Wayne, hard on the heels of rustlers, or an Indian maiden galloping bareback on her spirited paint, being pursued by the enemy.

Pounding hooves, flying manes, nostrils flaring in the wind, at night your saddle a pillow, and stars peppering a black sky overhead. Isn't that what horsemanship is all about? Of course. Partly, anyway. But there is much more to horsemanship than leaping onto a horse's back and racing the storm. Horsemanship is also more than just owning a horse and having a stable, although certainly they are convenient to have. Ownership in itself cannot make a horseman or horsewoman. Horsemanship requires dedication, deep interest in, and a true love for horses. It comes with knowing horses.

This knowing should include a bit of the history and development of the horse—how it grew into its present-day form. The horse was not always the same shape and size it is today. Some fifty or sixty million years ago, the ancestor of today's modern horse was called the "dawn horse," or by scientists the *Eohippus*. It was a somewhat ungainly little animal scarcely larger than a jackrabbit. *Eohippus* shared steamy swamplands with members of the dinosaur family. It sloshed around on padded feet, with four toes on its front feet and three on each hind foot. *Eohippus* had only one defense from its enemies—fleetness of foot. And in order to survive, it kept constantly alert and ready to run at the threat of danger.

After about twenty million years of development and adaptation to its changing environment, *Eohippus*'s legs lengthened and strengthened, and its speed increased accordingly. So did its size, and it grew to be as big as a goat. It became smarter and more alert, and its eyes moved to each side of its head, giving it much broader vision.

At this stage in its evolution, the horse became known

14

as the *Mesohippus,* or "middle horse." During this time many other changes were taking place. The swamps began to dry up, forming broad plains of hard ground. *Mesohippus* no longer needed its padded feet and spreading toes to muck around in the marshes. So its side toes, now useless, began to move up and out of the way. At the same time, the center toes gradually grew larger and more suited to running over hard ground. Millions of more years passed.

Discovered over a hundred years ago in Central Asia,
Przhevalski's horse is the only true wild horse
still in existence.

The creature's eating habits slowly changed from nibbling the leaves of swamp foliage to eating the grass that covered the broad plains in profusion. The larger *Mesohippus* became, the longer the distance it needed to stretch to reach down to the grass while remaining on its feet and alert to peril. As an adaptation to its grazing habits, the horse's neck grew longer. It also developed new and stronger teeth with which to graze on grass. After a few more million years *Mesohippus* grew and developed into the recognizable, hard-hoofed forerunner of the modern horse, *Equus*.

But many more thousands of years went by before any thought was given to taming or riding *Equus*. Early horses were hunted for food and their hides, not to be tamed. Nor is there any record of when or where man first got the idea or courage to hitch a horse to a sled or a wheeled vehicle, much less to leap aboard him and take what must have been one of the wilder rides in history.

Primitive drawings and crude statuary indicate that five thousand or so years ago the horse had become somewhat domesticated in parts of the world, particularly around the eastern edge of the Mediterranean Sea, and in the area stretching from Southeast Asia to sections of North Africa. In fact, thousands of years ago

Arabs originated selective breeding of best-stud-to-best-mare in order to improve the quality of their herds. The Arabian is the oldest pure breed of horse known, and there is Arabian horse blood, in some degree, in all domesticated horse stock today.

Horses had scarcely been domesticated before man

Arabian horse

found ways to use them in warfare. Someone developed the bit, a device by which horses could be better controlled. In Egypt, Syria, and India horses were hitched to chariots and driven into battle, spreading havoc among the enemy foot soldiers.

The use of war horses spread quickly to Europe. Greeks and Romans were some of the finest charioteers, as well as warriors on horseback. In medieval England, horses were bred for size and strength in order to carry knights sheathed in hundreds of pounds of armor. They were forerunners of today's heavy draft horses, such as the Clydesdale and Percheron.

Although other parts of the world had long been making full use of horses in both war and peace, there were no horses in North America when the Pilgrims landed on Plymouth Rock in 1620. They had disappeared about ten thousand years earlier and had not reappeared.

There were a few horses in nearby Mexico, however, brought into the area by the Spanish adventurer, Hernando Cortés, in the year 1519. The native Aztecs had never seen horses and were terrified by them. With this advantage, Cortés's mounted soldiers rode roughshod over the Indians and within a year conquered the rich land.

Percheron

In time, escaped or abandoned horses from Cortés's herd found their way northward. A couple of decades later a mounted army led by Francisco Coronado, a fellow countryman of Cortés, invaded the southeast areas of Arizona and New Mexico. In the years that followed, these Spanish horses of mixed breeds became

19

the ancestors of the vast herds of Western wild horses known as mustangs.

After the American Indians got over their initial amazement and fear at the sight of horses and mounted soldiers, they wanted some for themselves. They managed to get them by whatever means were available and, like the white man, were soon hunting, fighting, and traveling on horseback.

The West was settled and developed largely from the saddle.

Meanwhile, other horses had arrived by ship along the Eastern seaboard, and they were being bred and trained for the many tasks at hand. Some were used for pleasure riding, but most pulled farm equipment or buggies, or they were ridden with more purpose than simple enjoyment. Used for plowing, towing canal barges, pulling stagecoaches, herding cattle, and carrying the pony-express mail, horses played a critical role in the development of the nation.

In addition, Thoroughbreds and Hackneys had been imported from England, plus other fine horses from Hungary, Spain, and even Russia, which has more horses than any country in the world. (A Thoroughbred, incidentally, is a particular breed of horse, not to be confused with horses of other breeds that also have unmixed blood lines. Such horses are called purebreds and, like Thoroughbred horses, are registered generation by generation.)

By the beginning of the twentieth century there were approximately twenty million horses in the United States. Many were simply mixed strains. Yet from certain carefully controlled mixtures emerged such light but sturdy stock as the Morgan and the famous American quarter horse.

Other breeds of light horses that were developed in

the United States include the pinto, palomino, Appaloosa, buckskin, Saddlebred, and even the high-stepping, smoothly gaited Tennessee Walking Horse, which was used by Southern plantation owners to ride around their extensive cotton and tobacco lands. The Standardbred, or American trotter, used in harness racing is another famous American horse. It, like the Morgan, the quarter horse, and several less notable breeds of riding stock, is well endowed with Thoroughbred blood.

With the advent of the machine age, of course, the

American quarter horse

Tennessee Walking Horse

need for horses decreased dramatically. Their numbers
dwindled in the United States to about three million
animals. And, since the draft horse had given way to
the truck and tractor, most of the remaining stock were
light horses best suited for pleasure—parade horses,
polo ponies, hunters, jumpers, trail horses, racers, rodeo
mounts, and park riding horses.

And again another change took place. Riding and caring for horses became such a popular and pleasant pastime that the demand for horses began once more to increase. This increase has continued up to the present. Today there are approximately six million horses in the United States, and the number is steadily growing. There are horses of all sizes, colors, dispositions, and talents—a horse for anyone who really wants to ride.

Many sports and competitions are dependent upon the domesticated horse.

chapter two

CHOOSING A HORSE

As a young horse fancier, one of your biggest jobs, as well as an exciting pleasure, is choosing the right horse for your needs. You will surely spend some restless nights as you try to decide between an Appaloosa gelding, a quarter-horse mare, Morgan filly, pinto, or, indeed, the Shetland pony.

You are worried that all will be lost if you should happen to choose the wrong horse. Relax. Horse trading is a common practice in equestrian circles. The horse that you choose as a beginner probably will not be suited to your needs when you become a more advanced rider. And later, as an expert rider, you may find yourself looking around for a still more highly tuned and sensitive horse.

There is a constant turnover in horses, and neither horse nor rider need suffer for it. Although you surely will form strong attachments to any horse that serves you well, a part of horsemanship is to be able to part with a mount when the proper time comes for a change.

In your search for the right horse, the first rule is to

take your time. Six months is not unusual. Looking around increases your chances of locating the correct horse for your immediate needs.

Before going out to look for a horse, first ask yourself a few questions. How will you be using the horse? Do you intend simply to hack around the neighborhood? Would you care to ride in parades or show your horse in the ring? Or do you like the idea of entering in more demanding events such as hunting and jumping competition? Perhaps your ambitions may involve more rugged Western activities such as calf roping or barrel racing. Such things should be considered, for, although most horses are capable of performing in more than one

If you want to try jumping,
you will need a well-trained mount.

type of activity, every horse has special skills in certain areas of riding or showing.

Consider what price range you can afford. The cost in itself may prevent you from purchasing a sleek young Thoroughbred with a long registry of famous ancestors to its credit. Such "papered" horses usually are quite expensive and are not necessarily better riding horses. In fact, most horses being ridden for pleasure are of mixed blood. A mixed-breed horse sometimes brings out the finer features of each breed.

Horses whose blood lines have long since ceased to be traced are called stock, or grade, horses, and they make up the largest class of riding horses in existence. Although they have no pedigrees, they are normally just as loyal, just as good to ride, and just as much fun to own and care for as any blue-blooded purebred in the equine register. They certainly are less expensive. Healthy, sturdy, and well-trained purebred horse stock generally is priced in the thousands of dollars. On the other hand, a decent grade horse may be purchased for as little as a couple of hundred dollars.

In your search for the right horse, check ads in the newspapers and horse journals. Visit a breeding farm or horse dealer. Riding schools often put well-trained mounts up for sale. Occasionally you may even run across a horse auction where private owners often sell horses.

In the beginning, at least, don't concern yourself with blood lines. Be more concerned with size, temperament, general health, and the amount and kind of training the horse may have had.

If you are small, don't start out with a large sixteen-hand-high horse. (A hand is equal to four inches. A horse is measured from the ground to the highest point of the withers. A horse that is 15:2 is fifteen hands two inches tall, or sixty-two inches.) An animal under 14:2 hands, fifty-eight inches, is classified as a pony.

In fitting rider to horse, a rule of thumb is that, when mounted, the rider's heels should reach approximately to the bottom of the horse's rib cage, or the girth line. Your thighs, knees, and upper part of your calves should then rest comfortably against the horse. Having feet too high up on the horse's side or dangling below his barrel spoils the balance and proportion of rider and horse.

Having considered the general type of riding in which you are interested, plus the price and size of horse that you can best handle, you should then turn your attention to the physical and emotional traits of the horse.

When shopping for a horse, get all the information you can from the owner. Consider its age. A horse is in

28

its prime from about four to eight years of age. Most well-trained horses suitable for beginning riders are from around six to twelve years old and in good condition. A well-cared-for, twelve-year-old horse can not only look beautiful, it can possess lots of power and still be safe and dependable. A gelding (a neutered stallion) makes one of the best riding horses. A mare (a female horse over four years old) is usually good to ride and may one day even present you with a foal to raise. (A foal is any newborn horse less than a month old.)

A filly (a female horse under four years old) or a colt (a male horse under four years old) is seldom trained enough or settled down sufficiently to be suitable for a young, inexperienced rider.

A stallion seldom makes a decent riding horse for anyone, except an experienced trainer or a serious horse breeder.

So, if you are a novice rider, you are better off beginning with an older, well-ridden, fully trained, and dependable mount. Save the hot-blooded, high-stepping steeds for a later day when your riding skills are up to the challenge.

Find out the amount and type of training the horse has had. Is it more accustomed to the English saddle and the hunting and jumping types of activity? Or has its experience been under Western tack for trail riding, show ring, or rodeo? Many horses are trained for both English and Western styles of riding. If your mount has been trained to hunt and jump as well as trail ride and perform in other areas of equitation, you have a bonus horse.

Once you have talked things over with the seller and have at least a fair knowledge of the animal's background and training, you should make a closer inspection of the animal. Stand well back and look the horse over. Walk around it, and take in the general view. Visualize how it will look on the trail or in the show

parts of a horse

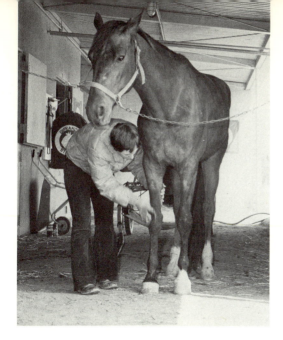

Pay particular attention
to the soundness of a horse's legs.

ring with you on its back. Is its general conformation good? Does it have a good head, properly proportioned, and held decently high out on a long neck? Most light horse breeds have a flat or slightly concave face rather than the Roman nose so often found on heavier draft horses.

The back should be short, with smoothly muscled thighs and sloping shoulders blending easily into flanks and neck. Legs should be sturdy and squarely set beneath the horse. Take particular notice of the knees and lower legs, where most soundness problems originate.

A deep, wide chest and a well-rounded girth indicate good lungs and heart and, consequently, fine endurance. Does its coat have the smoothness and bright sheen that typifies proper grooming and overall good health?

Make the first survey from a short distance, then move in for a close study. Always approach from a front quarter so as not to startle the animal. Look at its eyes. Are they large, alert, and wide apart, indicating intelligence? Wave your hand back a short distance beyond its normal line of sight. The horse should blink, indicating a full range of vision.

Are its ears small and upright, showing friendliness and a healthy curiosity? Or does it lay them back when you approach, indicating annoyance, suspicion, or anger? Does it twitch his ears or switch its tail a lot, signaling nervousness? Check its teeth. Although you may not be experienced enough in horse trading to read them properly for exact age, you can see if they are sound, not overly worn, not deeply grooved, and not slanted sharply forward, and so get a fairly accurate idea whether the horse is of good riding age.

After the horse has come to accept your touch and presence, run your hands down its legs. Pay particular attention to any unusual bumps or touchy spots. Check hooves to determine whether they have been properly trimmed and shod. Inspect the frog, that triangular-shaped cushion inside the bottom of the hoof. If healthy, it will be fairly soft and pliable, not dry and cracked.

While doing so, keep a sharp eye out for blemishes and unsoundnesses. A blemish is any abnormality that does not really affect the soundness of the horse. A wire cut that has properly healed, a rope burn that has left a minor scar, or a few warts may be unsightly, but they do not make the horse any less rideable.

On the other hand, if, for example, the horse heaves and wheezes, has an overly paunchy belly, is sway-backed, or has bowed tendons, he may be unfit for decent riding and certainly is not show-horse caliber.

You can often spot blemishes, but locating points of unsoundness usually is a task for experts. Unless you are completely sure that the horse you are considering buying is sound and healthy in every respect, you would do well to spend the nominal fee charged by a veterinarian of good repute to make a thorough check of the animal. X rays may be called for to determine the extent or seriousness of any abnormalities.

Before going that far, however, delve more deeply into the horse's general behavior. It may seem placid enough standing there as you look it over, but what happens when someone approaches it with a rope or

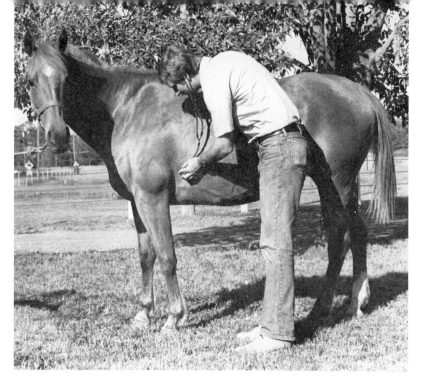

Having a vet check out the animal
is inexpensive insurance for the buyer.

halter? Does the horse seem to like the idea of companionship or of going for a ride? Or does it flatten its ears and prepare to run off, or does it stand its ground and wait for a chance to nip the intruder?

Is it touchy around the ears? Does it fight the bit? When it is finally haltered or bridled, does it lead easily? Such reactions of a horse to human contact give a good indication of its overall disposition.

The horse's behavior pattern is never more evident

than when it is being saddled. An improperly trained or mistreated horse becomes uneasy as soon as it sees someone approach with a saddle. It shies away when the saddle is lifted toward its back, fidgets or kicks, and becomes wholly uncooperative in accepting the cinch.

Once the horse is saddled and bridled, ask the owner to ride it while you stand back and watch. You can be sure the seller will try to show the horse off to best advantage. So look carefully and see how it handles. Does the animal run well? If gently reined, it probably has a good mouth, which has not been abused by jerks and hard pulls on the bit. Notice if it stops under only slight pressure. Does the horse back up straight to the rear as it should, not curling its backbone or stepping sideways?

See how well it walks, trots, and canters under its owner's hand. You might even ask the owner to let the horse out into a full gallop, if space permits. Watch how controllable the animal remains. Many an untrained horse, once its speed is up, tends to toss its head, ignore the bit, and race for the horizon. A properly trained horse will keep calm, mind its rider, and slow down easily to a walk.

The gallop also serves another purpose. Upon its return, pay attention to the depth and frequency of

After you have observed its mannerisms and temperament, try the horse out yourself.

the horse's breathing. Tune your ears to any unusual whistles or wheezes. See if it is foamed with sweat after the run. Common sense will dictate whether or not the horse is overly heated for the amount of exercise. A sound horse should handle a demonstration ride with cool ease.

Now take your turn in the saddle. Even if you are a beginner, any horse you would consider buying now should be calm enough, properly trained, and sufficiently dependable for your pleasure and safety.

36

Approach the horse with confidence, for it will be the first to detect any uncertainty in your mannerisms, and will be quick to take advantage of it. Given the upper hand, it will show disdain by making your entire ride difficult.

Once in the saddle, however, put it through its paces with firm patience. Rein in both directions to see whether it responds equally well to the right and left. Ride it close alongside a fence or corral railing to see if it shies away. If you have a solid enough seat and ample experience, you might wave your hat or create deliberate confusion to see whether or not it spooks easily. See how smoothly it shifts from walk to trot to slow gallop or canter. The mount should be sensitive to both the reins and bit, but not overly "quick" or it may unseat you.

If your check ride proves satisfactory, you are well along to making your decision whether or not to buy the animal. But don't hurry it! No horse is perfect. Look around for a horse trailer, and see how your prospective horse takes to it. At least, see if it leads in obediently and backs out willingly. If it doesn't balk at those stages, it will probably trailer well.

Go with the horse when it is being returned to the stable. Does it lead in and out of the stall with equal cooperation? While there, check the bedding material for the amount of food waste in it. Of course, uneaten fodder is not necessarily a sign of a finicky or careless eater; he may simply have been overly fed. Also, if you haven't had the opportunity earlier, observe whether recent manure is solid and made up basically of roughage.

Even if you seem satisfied with one particular horse, don't hesitate to look around a little more. As a potential buyer you may be inclined to become attached to just about any horse that gives you a doleful look with his big, bright eyes. Yet if you end your search at once, you may miss a better horse at a more attractive price just a half mile down the road.

Even while shopping around, go back several times to have another look at the horse or horses you favor. See the horse in the cool of early morning when it's full of pepper. See it during feeding time. Notice whether it plays with the food or if it eats hungrily. See the horse when it's tired and inclined to droop a bit. Get to know it better—and under all conditions—before you plunk down your first payment. Sure, there's always a little concern that someone else may grab the horse. But nine times out of ten by taking your time you'll end up with the right horse for you.

Usually an experienced equestrian should be along

when you are getting ready to make a decision. Though less official and skilled than the veterinarian, who will make the most important check, your horseman friend may observe things with a cool, detached eye that you in your enthusiasm have failed to note. He will at least have the chance to see whether you and the horse are suited for each other in matters of experience, temperament, and riding styles.

With the proper knowledge of what you are looking for, with sufficient care and patience in seeking it, and, indeed, with a little outside help, you will surely find the right horse to ride and care for.

chapter three

CARE AND FEEDING

Always keep in mind that your horse is a living, feeling, and thinking friend, not a mere machine. It needs basically the same things you need—shelter, food and water, exercise, good grooming, and health care. To provide the basic essentials necessary to maintain an attractive and healthy horse, you must devote a lot of time, hard work, and some money to the job.

You must be willing to accept these responsibilities and expenses before you buy a horse. Of course, many young horse owners work out an agreement with their parents, often on a basis of "I'll give my horse tender, loving care if you will help buy and support it."

Many horses are boarded at private stables or riding clubs established largely for that purpose. Although this arrangement relieves you of much work and responsibility, it usually is quite expensive, as high as one hundred dollars a month at a good stable. Such a stable may be quite a distance from your home, making difficult the daily contact with your horse that is so desirable. On the other hand, if you don't live where there are ample room and facilities to raise and train a horse, a boarding stable is your best bet.

Of course, many horse lovers are in no position to own their own horses. Yet they can satisfy their desires to ride, and even help groom and care for a horse, by going to a rental stable and getting acquainted with both the manager and the horses. Doing so is particularly wise before you decide to own your own horse.

Assuming, however, that you have a horse and live out of town where there is sufficient space to raise and ride it, you have plenty to keep you busy. You might first consider the horse's safety and comfort. Although your horse will and should spend a large part of its idle time outdoors at pasture or in a paddock, it also needs protection from too much heat, cold, rain, snow, insect pests, and such. Thus, a stable is usually called for.

Stables can be of any size or design, as long as certain needs are met. A stable may be nothing more than a properly walled, roofed, lighted, and ventilated stall. Or it may be made up of several stalls under a single roof. Ideally it has a hay and grain storage area adjacent to the stalls, plus a tack room for saddles and riding equipment nearby.

Each box stall should be about twelve feet square, allowing ample room for your horse to move around,

Most horse lovers have to settle for a less ideal setup
than this one to raise and ride their horses.

lie down, or roll as it sees fit. It should have a high ceil-
ing, preferably nine feet or more. There should be at
least one window, which swings out to let air in and yet
can be closed on cold winter nights. The glass, if any,
should be protected by strong wire mesh. For the purpose of cross ventilation, the window should be placed
toward the rear of the stall, opposite the four-foot-wide,
two-part Dutch stable doors.

It is important that the stable be built on high ground
where there is good drainage. Many stables have clay

or dirt floors, which is fine as long as they are kept reasonably dry. A bedding of shavings or straw would help maintain this dryness. Wood or paved floors are acceptable, although wood is noisy and inclined to retain unpleasant odor and to splinter. If the floor is paved, extra amounts of bedding material must be provided for your horse's comfort.

The walls and doors of the stable must be strongly built of heavy timbers in case your horse starts kicking. If your mount is a wood nibbler, you may also need to protect exposed edges of posts and planking with strips of metal or some other protective covering. Sometimes creosote paint or some types of chemical repellents discourage nibbling. Many efficient stables are constructed of concrete blocks.

For healthy and efficient feeding, there should be some sort of a hayrack in the stall. There should also be a grain-feeder tub of some kind. Certainly a ready supply of clean water is important. Most modern stables use automatic dispensers, whereby the horse nuzzles a small paddle to fill a small bowl with whatever water it may want.

The stable should be easy to clean, and there should be someplace away from the building to store manure until it is disposed of. Cleanliness is one of the most important chores in proper stable management. You must turn over the bedding each day, removing manure and all wet and soiled material. Then provide clean shavings, straw, or whatever you use for bedding. To allow waste materials to collect day after day is to invite flies and subsequent health problems, which rob much of the joy of owning a horse. The careful, considerate horse owner will keep everything clean and sanitary on a day-to-day basis.

Feeding is another major factor in raising a horse. It is also the single most expensive item. The variety of diets and the conditions under which you must decide how much of which type of food to give your horse are endless. For instance, if your horse is put out to pasture and the grass is both succulent and plentiful, your horse can loaf through days or even weeks of getting along nicely without any food supplements. There should, of course, be a salt lick available and plenty of good water. Both are critical to your horse's health.

On the other hand, if you start riding and working your horse, regardless of how good the pasturage is, you should add some grain to its diet. Grain is the main source of energy. Oats, bran, and in some regions corn are the most common types of grains fed to horses. The amount fed each horse depends largely upon the weight

Horses often need food supplements
to go with hay and grain.

of the horse and the amount of work it is doing. A horse
doing normal work will get by nicely on less than a half
pound of grain for each hundred pounds of body weight.
That is, four or five pounds of grain per day for a
thousand-pound horse.

Where pasturage is skimpy, or nonexistent, feed your
horse regular rations of good quality hay. It needs the
roughage and the natural minerals and vitamins con-

tained in the hay. Usually you should feed at least part of the hay first to take the edge off your horse's appetite, so it won't gobble the grain to follow. You should give it about the amount of loose hay or portions of baled hay that it will eat in a half hour or so. The best hays are alfalfa, timothy, and clover. If you overfeed the horse, it may get an undesirable hay belly or too much fat over the ribs. Be sure the hay is good quality, free from weeds or sticks and not dusty or moldy.

It is important that you put your horse on a regular feeding schedule. If you are not working your horse hard, two feedings a day should do. Feed half his ration in the morning and the remainder at night. If you are riding a lot, you might divide his rations in thirds, giving him fairly equal amounts morning, noon, and evening. Always feed the horse early enough to allow at least a partial digestion of the food before working it.

There are many brands of commercial horse feeds on the market. Extremely popular are the pellets that contain all the necessary food ingredients—hay, grain, vitamins, minerals, the works. They are usually more expensive than baled hay and sacked oats, however, but they are extremely convenient and there is very little waste. Some pellets are no larger than marbles; others are the size of ping-pong balls or hockey pucks. Size and shape are of little consequence, as long as the ingredients are balanced and nutritious. Even when you use all-purpose quickly eaten pellets, you should usually supplement them with a little hay so your horse has something to munch on as it whiles away its leisure time.

Just like people, horses can be either finicky eaters or good eaters. You must feed your horse according to what you observe it wants or needs. If it is alert and seems content, if it has the glow of health and its ribs are sheathed beneath smoothly fleshed skin, you probably are giving it the right amounts of the proper foods. If it is thin, shaggy, and its head droops, make some changes in its diet. It may need a vitamin supplement. Usually, short of having to consult a veterinarian, you can get some good counsel from your feed-store manager, an experienced horseman friend, or a stable owner. By observing your horse and using common sense, you should have little difficulty keeping it properly fed.

The keenness of its appetite and the overall well-being of its functioning body parts—stomach, intestines, bowels—will depend largely upon your horse getting plenty of exercise. Having a pasture in which you can turn it loose to romp is helpful. Then it can take pretty good care of itself between rides. But without such a pasture, your duty, as well as pleasure, is to take it out

A mechanical "hot walker" can be used
for exercising or cooling down a horse.

for exercise. Ride your horse, walk it, chase it. Just be
sure that, one way or another, you exercise it regularly
and vigorously enough to make it break a sweat and get
comfortably tired. You can work your horse in circles
out on the end of a thirty-foot-long rein, called a "longe
line." Or you can even resort to attaching it to a me-
chanically run hot walker, an automatic merry-go-
round-like contraption that can be used both for exercising or for cooling down a horse after a strenuous
workout on the trail or in the arena.

48

No less important than feeding and exercising is the daily grooming of your horse. You can do most of it yourself. Parts of it you must let others do and pay for their services.

For instance, there is no part of a horse more important than its hooves. A horse's shoes wear out. Its hard hooves seldom grow evenly. They must be trimmed and reshod regularly by an expert farrier, or blacksmith. With the big increase in riding horses during the past decade or so, many new farriers have taken up the once-dying trade of horseshoeing. They usually travel around in pickup or panel trucks loaded with iron-bar stock, nails, a heavy anvil, hammers and tongs, and a portable propane-fueled forge.

You need the services of a good farrier about every six to eight weeks, depending upon how hard you have been working your horse. Even if you haven't been riding, and the shoes aren't badly worn, in six or so weeks the hooves grow out of proportion to them. This condition may throw the horse off balance and put extra strain on its tendons. The skilled farrier, through proper trimming of the hoof and careful forging and fitting of a shoe to each foot, is able to maintain your horse's firm and proper underpinning. In addition, a reputable horseshoer has a thorough knowledge of the physiology of a

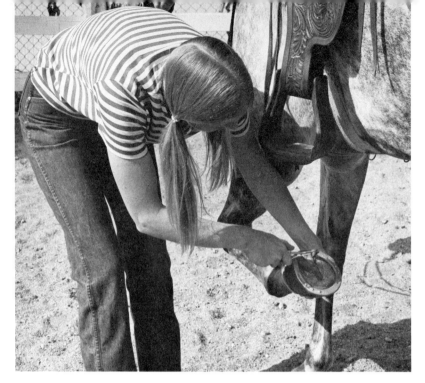

Use the hoof pick to clean around the frog.

horse's legs and feet, and he is able to correct certain defects in movement by proper trimming and shoeing. Be a friend to your farrier, for he will have a great deal to do with keeping healthy feet under your horse.

Of course, there is much you can do about hoof care also. Each day you should inspect all four hooves and, with your hoof pick, clean out any dirt, manure, stones, or other matter that may have packed or wedged inside the hoof wall or around the padded, v-shaped frog. While so doing you can also check for cracks or any

50

signs of infection. Dry and brittle hooves can be helped by using a hoof oil or a commercial hoof dressing.

Keeping the ground inside the corral sprinkled down during hot, dry weather will also help restore or maintain the moisture in the hoof. Your farrier, although not a professional medical man, is well equipped to alert you should your horse's hooves need more or a different kind of care than they have been getting.

For actual medical problems, you will need the services of a trained veterinarian. If you keep your facilities clean and sanitary, provide good shelter, proper food, and see that your horse gets enough exercise, chances are that you will not need any emergency service from the vet. Still, he should check even a healthy horse once a year. While on the scene, he or she will provide the annual flu and tetanus shots and worm your horse. All horses are susceptible to worms; most have at least a few. The veterinarian will determine whether they need medicinal control or not. Your vet also will check the heartbeat, breathing, temperature, and the vital functions of your horse. Indeed, through observation and early prevention, the annual visit of your veterinarian may save you money.

You can also save money by doing a number of things personally to keep your horse attractively groomed and healthy. The two basic times for grooming are just before and fairly soon after the ride. This means cleaning your horse from hooves to head and brushing it down well.

If your horse is particularly dirty, you should use a currycomb first, preferably the more gentle rubber comb, instead of a metal one. Use it to remove loose hair and dirt. Start on the left side (called the "near" side in horse parlance). Curry the neck, chest, shoulders, foreleg down to the knee, back, side, belly, and hind legs down to the hock. Don't use the rather hard currycomb on sensitive areas around the head or below the knees or hocks. Curry with a circular motion, and use as light a pressure as will still get the horse clean. Knock the dirt and hair out of the comb frequently.

Follow the currying with a brisk brushing with a stiff-fibered dandy brush. Brush with the grain of the hair, so the blanket or saddle will rest comfortably on your horse's back, and be sure the cinch area is clean. Be careful when brushing around the sensitive parts of the face, ears, and the tender insides of the legs. Don't just hit the high spots. Get around the tail, under the belly, and to all the hard-to-reach areas. Comb the mane and tail. Get the kinks, twists, and burrs out of the long hair, and follow up with a good brushing. You can't groom a horse properly standing straight up. Bend and search and talk to your horse as you work. Move slowly so you won't surprise or startle it.

Now take the softer body brush—your most important grooming tool—and brush your horse's entire body. It will like the gentle brushing, which gives a healthy sheen to its already clean coat. Again, brush with the grain of the hair and just as long as you want. Your horse won't mind a bit.

You can polish the whole cleaning operation off with a grooming cloth. Any two-foot-square piece of old toweling or blanket makes a worthy grooming cloth. With it give a final polish to your horse's coat. Also hit places you haven't touched before. Wipe its eyes and ears, lips and nostrils, and around the tail. Touch up your horse with the same pride you would if it were an expensive foreign sports car, or, indeed, with more pride, for it is a flesh-and-blood friend.

Other grooming tools you will need include a hoof pick and a sweat scraper to remove excessive perspiration from a heated animal following a ride. Often a dry rag can be used for the same purpose. If the day is warm and sunny, a good washdown is an excellent way to groom your horse totally.

When you're all finished, look it over. If you like

what you see, clean up your grooming tools and put them away. If it's getting chilly, put a blanket over the animal. Then lead it to the stall where you may already have set out its dinner.

Look past the halter. If you have been taking proper care of your horse, groomed it carefully, and given it the affection that it needs, you should be able to see a smile of contentment on its equine face.

Most horses appreciate a warm-weather washdown.

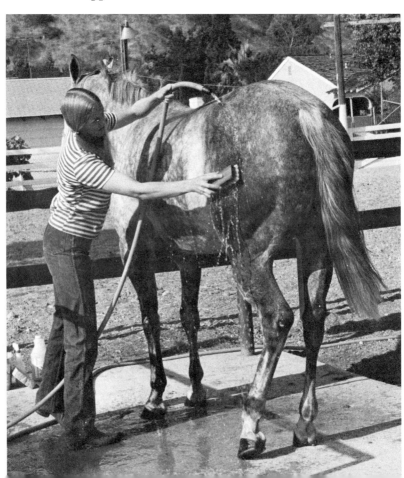

chapter four

TACK

Tack is any or all of the paraphernalia that you put on your horse for the sake of control, comfort, training, and decoration. Common items of tack are saddles, blankets, pads, bridles, halters, hackamores, girths (called a "cinch" in Western riding), martingales, breast collars, to name a few.

The variety, quality, and cost of tack are wide-open subjects. For instance, you can buy a simple working halter of braided rope for a few dollars. Or you can get a finely embossed top-grain leather halter full of silver pieces for a hundred dollars or more. You can choose a very inexpensive saddle blanket made from reused fibers, or you can provide your horse with an expensive custom-sewn saddle pad or a genuine Navajo blanket. And on and on.

Often when you buy a horse, you have the opportunity to purchase some of the tack that goes with it. This arrangement is fine for the horse if the tack fits it properly, since it is accustomed to the gear. However, it may be wrong for you. The saddle may be too short in the seat, cramping your ability to adjust to varying riding conditions. A bridle with a simple curb bit may not afford you enough control. Or the item of tack may be a type you are unfamiliar with, such as a hackamore, a halter that has no bit. Wherever possible, try to test out pieces of tack before making a purchase. Most private owners and some tack shops will let you do so. A reliable saddlery will give you much valuable assistance in choosing proper tack. If you are considering second-hand equipment and are unsure of its quality or price, seek the counsel of an experienced horseman. Giving advice is part of the fun and friendliness between fellow horse fanciers.

Nowhere is the variation in quality and price more evident than in saddles, which will invariably be your first concern once you have your horse. The two main styles of saddles in widespread use today are the simple English saddle and the heavier Western stock, or work, saddle.

The English saddle is fine for cross-country and bridle-trail riding. It also is the saddle designed for hunting and jumping and show-ring equitation. In past years, the English saddle was used mostly in the Eastern part of the country. However, it is now just as popular in the West.

A light saddle with a low profile, the English saddle has no horn on the pommel and a low rear cantle. By far the most popular English saddle used today is known as the "forward seat," so called because the rider's weight is moved up and forward over the animal's withers where it is most capable of carrying it. This position is generally preferred to the one in which the rider sits in the middle of the horse's back in the so-called classic, or "saddle seat."

The English saddle uses a single leather girth. It has simple metal stirrups (irons) held by plain stirrup straps (leathers). It has rather small rounded side flaps, often

parts of the English saddle

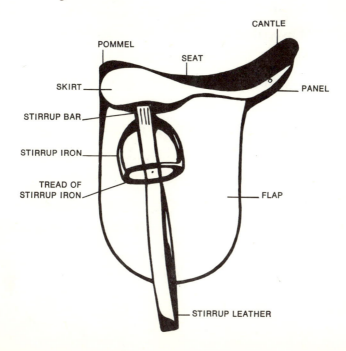

with padded knee rolls along the forward edge. These rolls give you extra support when riding or jumping in a forward position. In recent years, however, there has been a strong trend away from the padded rolls, so you now must ride with extra skill in order to keep your proper seat.

The second major type of saddle is the Western stock saddle. It is the saddle that fills TV and movie screens as cowboys gallop through cactus-filled canyons or flee from showers of Indian arrows.

Whereas the English saddle is basically a stripped-down flat pad that doesn't do much more than support a pair of stirrups, the stock saddle is a Western rider's home-on-horseback. It is a working saddle, designed as much for ranch and rodeo work as for show-ring riding.

The Western saddle has a deep, comfortable seat situated between a high pommel at the front and a high cantle at the rear. The pommel has an upthrust horn topped off by a rounded knob. This horn was originally designed to loop or dally a rope around in order to hold a lassoed steer, and it is still used for such on the range or in rodeos.

On the other end of the Western saddle seat there is also room behind the cantle to tie a bedroll, a slicker, and maybe even a frying pan or coffeepot.

The Western saddle has wide leather skirts. It is usually lined with sheepskin that rests comfortably along the back of the horse and distributes the weight of saddle and rider evenly. Heavy leather fenders against which your legs rest hang down each side, ending with the bold wood or leather-covered stirrups.

Western saddles often use a single cinch slung underneath the barrel of the horse directly behind his front legs. Some cowboys call this a "center-fire rig." However, in order to hold the saddle more securely in place

parts of the Western saddle

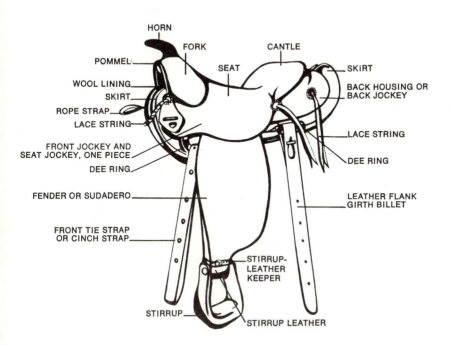

when roping cattle, most modern saddles are double rigged. That is, instead of one cinch they use two, one fabric cinch forward and a leather one in back. The back cinch is easily detachable, so a rider can decide which style best fits his own needs.

Whereas the style of English saddles emphasizes plainness, with a smooth, sleek, simple cut, and richly tanned leathers, the stock saddle often is more elaborate, with tooling, embossing, and leather carving. Some

Horse tacked out with a double-rigged Western saddle, breast collar, and bridle.

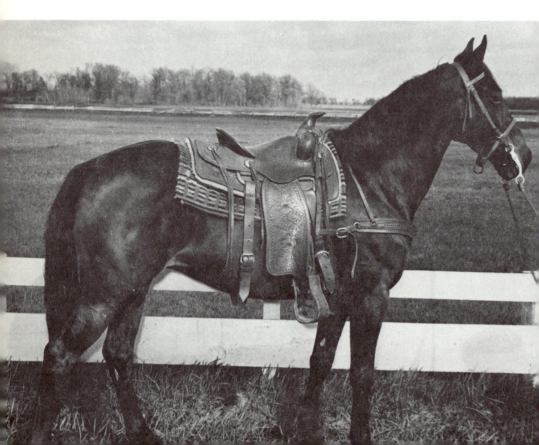

parade saddles are heavily ornamented with silver or stainless steel. Leather stitching, called "buckstitching," often adds to the appearance and value of a Western saddle.

Both types of saddles are manufactured in approximately the same manner. The foundation of each is a saddle tree. The saddle tree is an assembly of carefully carved pieces of wood that are shaped and glued together to fit comfortably onto a horse's back, while staying free of the sensitive backbone. Some saddle trees are formed of plastic. When possible, the tree should be fitted to the horse before the saddle maker gets to the finishing steps. But this customizing is often both inconvenient and expensive. Consequently, many saddle trees are made to fit particular breeds of horses having similar conformations, such as the Arab, Morgan, Thoroughbred, quarter horse, and such.

The saddle tree is covered with tight layers of leather or canvas. Instead of being completely rigid, it has a certain resiliency, allowing it to give a little under the bending and twisting motions during a ride.

In well-planned steps, skilled saddlers add padding, then cut and fit leather skirts, flaps, straps, and coverings to finish off the saddle. If the work has been done properly, and if you have taken care to see that the saddle fits both you and your horse comfortably and securely, you will have eliminated a few riding problems before they occur.

A good saddle will help keep you on your horse only if you are able to control it. Doing so is not always easy. You may weigh only a hundred or so pounds, while your horse weighs upward of a thousand pounds. It is larger and much stronger than you, and it does not always listen to reason. Obviously you need help in controlling the horse, help that is not unlike the power steering or power brakes in an automobile.

Your number one piece of equipment that provides this control is the bridle. Bridles are the most varied and complicated of all items of tack. The bridle is made up of a head harness, called a "headstall," a bit, and a set of reins. The headstall is an assembly of straps that fit over the horse's head and hold a metal bar, or bit, in his mouth. The reins attach to the ends of the bit. Pulling on the reins causes leverage on the bit. The pressure of the bit in the horse's mouth helps to convey your wish for it to slow down, turn, or stop.

There is a wide variety of sizes and shapes in bits, but two main types are commonly used in pleasure riding. The basic bit in English riding is the snaffle. It is made up of a single bar usually jointed in the middle. A large

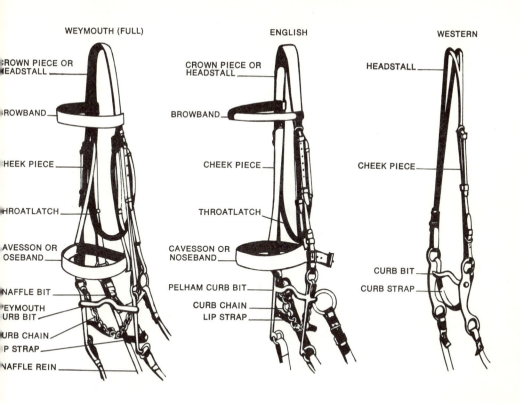

WEYMOUTH (FULL)   ENGLISH   WESTERN

CROWN PIECE OR HEADSTALL

BROWBAND

CHEEK PIECE

THROATLATCH

CAVESSON OR NOSEBAND

SNAFFLE BIT

WEYMOUTH CURB BIT

CURB CHAIN

LIP STRAP

SNAFFLE REIN

CROWN PIECE OR HEADSTALL

BROWBAND

CHEEK PIECE

THROATLATCH

CAVESSON OR NOSEBAND

PELHAM CURB BIT

CURB CHAIN

LIP STRAP

HEADSTALL

CHEEK PIECE

CURB BIT

CURB STRAP

basic types and parts of bridles

loop or ring is attached to each end, to which are fastened the headstall straps and reins. When you pull the reins on a snaffle bit, it exerts a direct but relatively gentle pressure on the horse's tongue and the corners of his mouth. The snaffle-equipped bridle, with its single set of reins, is simple to operate and preferred by most beginning riders.

63

More skilled English-style riders may use a Pelham bridle for added control. The Pelham has a single bit, but a double set of rings to which are attached double sets of reins. That is, you have four reins to handle instead of two. Although more difficult to handle, double reins do afford more positive control over your horse.

If you are a Western-style rider, you will prefer using a curb bit. The curb is a solid bar and is slightly more severe than a snaffle. The curb bit has an upward bend, or port, in its middle. Attached to each end of the bit is

A variety of bits can be used
with most headstalls to make up a bridle.

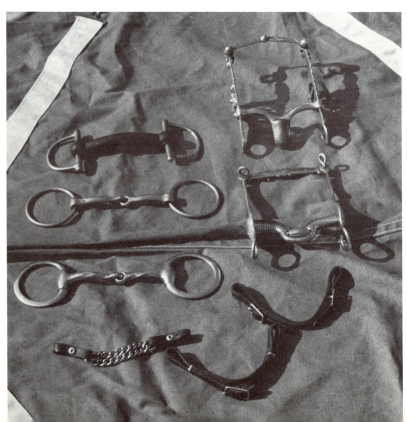

a metal cheek piece with a pair of loops, top and bottom. The headstall and curb strap attach to the top loops. The reins attach to the bottom loops.

By pulling on the reins of a curb-bitted bridle, you exert down-and-back leverage on the bit. This leverage puts pressure on the tongue and on the bars inside your horse's mouth. The bars are the tender spaces of tooth-less gum between your mount's incisor teeth and molars. The bar spaces are several fingers wide, affording ample room for the bit to rest on. Pulling the reins also tightens the curb strap, or chain, up under your horse's tender chin groove, which will make it heed your wishes even more willingly.

A somewhat complicated variation of a bridle is called the Weymouth. It is known as a full bridle, having two bits—both a snaffle and a curb—and requires a double set of reins. The Weymouth is used primarily by advanced riders on gaited show horses of the Saddle-bred class.

Despite a confusing variety of bridles, your choice should be one that fits your horse comfortably and will produce maximum obedience under the least amount of force. The primary skill of horsemanship is to be able to control your mount without the use of undue strength. Jerking on reins or otherwise overcontrolling will ruin a good mouth and abuse other tender pressure points so that in time the horse will no longer respond and become unmanageable.

In any decently supplied tack room you surely will find such items as quilted saddle pads and blankets used for softening the contact between the saddle and the horse's back. All of the grooming brushes and materials are also kept in the tack room. A large, fitted horse blanket should be available for protecting your horse from rain, cold, and biting insects. The same blanket will come in handy after a hard, sweaty ride. Put the blanket on your horse while you walk it around, or when it's hitched up to the hot-walker machine during the cooling-down period.

When bringing your horse in from pasture, tying it up, or simply leading it around, you need some kind of a halter. A halter is a simple assembly of leather or rope that fits loosely on the horse's head. It can remain in place even while the horse is eating or sleeping.

You also need a good lead line for moving your horse around. It can be rope, leather, braided rawhide, or webbing. It can be almost any length, although from five to seven feet is most practical. It should terminate on one end with an easy-to-work swivel snap for attaching it to the halter.

You do not ordinarily ride a horse using only a halter and lead rope, although you can do so sometimes if your horse is well trained and in a small arena or fenced pasture.

If you want to ride the trails without a bridle you might try using a hackamore halter. Although the hackamore doesn't have a bit, it does have reins and works on nose and chin pressure. A good dispositioned, properly trained horse usually will work well with a hackamore when being ridden for pleasure, even under demanding conditions.

A breast strap or breast collar, plain or fancy, is a handy item used to prevent the saddle from sliding back when on a hilly trail ride. The breast strap also can be used for attaching a martingale, a simple strap arrangement that fastens to the bridle and restrains the horse when it is inclined to throw its head up and back into your face. Both English and Western riders use breast collars.

No doubt you will have an extra set of reins or two— your practice reins and your show ring reins. And your show bridle may be extra-fine leather, double stitched, or even silver mounted. Sometimes such bridles are awarded, to most horse lovers' delight, in shows instead of ribbons, trophies, or plaques.

Be sure to have replacement pieces of riding equipment. In case something should break on your bridle or saddle, you can easily replace it, go on your ride, and save yourself a drive to the tack shop.

You will also want a longe line. Not only can you use it for exercising or cooling down your horse, you can use the line to train it to various gaits. Standing back at the end of the line, you can watch the horse's movements and cue it with voice commands or flicks of a switch. Longeing (or lunging) is very effective during early training, when the horse is too young to ride.

Your tack room may also contain equipment to protect your horse. Protective shipping boots and tail wraps are used when trailering a horse. You may include shin boots or skid boots used in Western stock-horse training. Splint boots and bell boots are used to protect jumpers. If your horse tends to spook easily, you may have a pair of simple blinkers to settle him down while trail riding.

All of these things are considered tack, and all require some care. Certainly everything must be kept clean. Some things, such as bits, should be regularly washed with soap and water and thoroughly rinsed. Leather goods should be treated occasionally with saddle soap or one of the many commercial leather dressings. Yet, depending upon usage, don't rub in oil too often, or the leather loses much of its strength and the stitching becomes weakened. Saddle soap is the most suitable product for general leather cleaning and care.

Your tack room should also contain a few horse-care items such as hoof dressing, fly spray, horse shampoo, and simple medications for minor cuts and scratches. Treatment of more serious conditions should be left to the veterinarian.

So, all in all, you might say the tack room is the control center of your stable. And your horse will perform pretty much in accordance with the type and quality of the equipment you use.

chapter five

RIDER'S DRESS

As an owner you are deeply proud of your horse and so take care to keep it in good health and looking its best. To be a good horseman or horsewoman, you must also be concerned with your own appearance. Are you neat, clean, and properly dressed for the riding occasion? Do you, in short, look the part?

If you are working around the stables, doing your daily grooming, or simply practicing around your own paddock as you prepare for a weekend show, you wouldn't, of course, wear your Sunday best. A T-shirt and denims are fine. Clothes are inclined to pick up corral dirt and horse smells around the stable. So save your good clothes for the trail ride or the show ring.

Entirely different styles of clothing are worn for Western and English riding. Western riders dress pretty much in the cowboy tradition, which is considerably more casual than English dress.

Properly close-fitting jeans are the most common foundation for the Western rider's garb. Tightness is essential, for loose pants will slide up, wrinkle, and chafe.

70

If you have a Western suit custom-made, stretch materials are very desirable. But most materials are acceptable as long as they are simple, fitted, and durable.

Keep in mind color coordination, not only for yourself but for your horse and its tack. Try to make all colors complement each other, so the overall appearance is a good one; then you will ride out as a sharp team.

If you enter Western shows, you will wear chaps over your pants. They are tightly fitted, fringed or unfringed, plain or decorated. The modern trend is toward the "shotgun" style—narrow chaps that wrap around the legs, fringed on the outside, with zippers up the sides, and a slight flare over the boot. Big "batwing" chaps are usually reserved for rodeo events and parades, or history books.

Western shirts come in great variety, quality, and price. They may be plain or embroidered, buttoned or snapped. They are usually yoked, and they should always have long sleeves. A Western show shirt should allow shoulder room for action, yet be tailored along the bodice, fit snugly around the waist, and have long tails so they won't come flying out during a competition ride. The shirt may be as colorful as you like, although if you are competing in an event, you want to have the

Full-leg "shotgun" chaps
are very much the Western style.

attention of the judge and audience focused on your horse and performance rather than on a flashy shirt.

Western riders often wear matching pants and shirt. Sometimes they are tailored one-piece suits, although wearing a belt makes them appear to be two-piece. They are comfortable to ride in and certainly eliminate any fear of shirttails flying, for there are none.

A Western rider probably takes greatest pride in his or her boots. Western boots are fairly low, coming only to the bottom or partway up the calf of the leg. They have high heels designed to keep the foot from slipping through the stirrup or to enable the rider to dig into the ground if he has a calf on the far end of his lariat.

Western boot styles still accept the traditional pointed toe, but squared-off and rounded boot toes provide added comfort. Heels also have changed somewhat during recent years, becoming less high. They are still high enough to perform their original functions, yet they have become low enough to make walking a bit easier and more graceful.

Your boots can be of any color or inlaid with several colors. Usually you will want some kind of decorative stitching worked into the leather tops. A good pair of top-grain leather boots can become the major investment of your riding attire and should be given the same care and attention you give your horse and saddle.

A high-crowned hat normally tops off your Western garb. There are also acceptable low-crowned hats, although they are less popular. The hat can be made of felt or straw, depending largely upon climate and season. It may have a plain or fancy hatband, again with the emphasis on plain. It should fit snugly and level over your forehead. There are few things more embarrassing or likely to lose points than to be in the middle of a riding event and have a slight gust of wind send your hat cartwheeling across the arena.

There are numerous accessories to go with your basic Western riding clothes. A broad belt, for instance, with a bold silver buckle, is very much a part of Western dress for both male and female riders. Normally you top off your shirt collar with a kerchief or a short tie. Both should be tucked in, pinned down, or be small enough so as not to flap in the breeze. Gloves add a fine finishing touch to Western garb, as well as having the added practical value of protecting your hands.

Spurs are, of course, very much a part of riding, both for looks and for subtle control of your horse. A well-trained horse does not generally need to be spurred. And even when you use spurs, the action should be a gentle nudge in the side, never a hard jab. In fact, most Western spurs today have small blunt rowels, not the big, sharp-tipped, brutal pinwheels that the villains wear in Western movies.

It is not permissible for the Western horsewoman to wear her hair long and loose in the show ring. It should be neat and secure, preferably braided or pulled back into a bun. Some girls prefer to comb it up and pin it beneath their hat. Here, again, the trend in your area, or the type of event you are riding in serves to dictate how your hair should be worn. For simply trail riding, long hair is okay.

So, all in all, there is a great deal of variety in Western dress. Take your time in making your choice, and get full comfort, pride, and pleasure from what you wear.

English-riding garb is considerably more formal, designed specifically for show riding. When you head out on the trails, however, you may wear pretty much the same things you do for informal Western riding.

When you are in the working ring, or on a weekend group ride in the park, you should doll yourself up in breeches or jodhpurs, a simple leather belt, a comfortable shirt, or perhaps a light turtleneck sweater. Your boots should go with the style leg covering you use. Breeches (commonly pronounced britches) fit inside your boots and require high-topped, full-leg boots. On the other hand, jodhpurs go over your boots, which are only ankle high. Straps of the jodhpurs go under your boot instep and keep the cuffs from creeping up your leg. Whereas breeches are usually close fitting from waist to ankle, jodhpurs (jods) are often flared at the hip. Yet, here again, current style has pretty much eliminated the flare. Today the most popular breeches are made of

Properly dressed for informal English riding.

close-fitting stretch materials, giving a trim look to both male and female riders. Colors vary from white to black, with gray, beige, and yellow often being worn.

To turn the leisurely trail-riding outfit of breeches

and boots into show-ring dress, you must add a formal coat, a fitted shirt with matching choker or stock tie and a hard hat. English-riding coats are varied and very stylish. Most commonly seen in the arena and on the park trail is the midlength coat, flared comfortably at the hips and split at the tail in order to spread properly when the rider is in the saddle. It is tailored to fit closely at the waist, have flap pockets, and button down the front with three or four high-placed buttons so as not to

Knee-high boots, breeches, a riding coat, and hunt cap
are proper dress for jumping and English equitation.

interfere with the flaring at the bottom. The coats come in assorted plaids and solid colors, all of which are acceptable, although navy, black, and brown seem to be the most popular. Tweeds, of course, are less likely to show dirt. These midlength coats are worn for hunting, jumping, and equitation classes.

A hard hat, or hunt cap, tops off the English show outfit. It has a hard protective crown, a small front visor, and a chin strap as a safety measure. The more formal types of gaited classes call for the formal, longer coats and a derby or, at times, a full top hat, jods, and jodhpur boots.

A riding vest is optional. Gloves are not required, but they add to your general appearance and are an aid in handling the reins. Light spurs with blunt tips are sometimes used for added control.

In English riding, your hair should be tied back or put up under your hat out of the way. This style makes for a neater appearance to go with the hunt cap. Certainly during hunting or jumping loose hair should not be flying around your face. Boys have less of a problem in this area, although while long male hair is in vogue, boy riders frequently tuck and pin their hair as well.

So, the amount, quality, and variety of riding attire is vast. Within the two major areas of Western and English riding you may find your mind churning with indecision, hoping to avoid a glaring mistake in the way you dress. Don't worry. You will have plenty of opportunities when you visit stables or attend riding events to see what others are wearing. What is being worn in one part of the country may be quite different from that worn in another. In general, bear in mind the current trends and you will have no problem.

A serious horseman or horsewoman dresses for the occasion, which is a good part of the fun of riding.

chapter six

TACK UP AND MOUNT

Sometimes you may rent a horse at a public stable. Or you may go on trail rides at summer camp. Dude-ranch horses are often kept busy by riders who don't own their own mounts. When you are a rider rather than a horse owner, you don't often get involved in "tacking up," as saddling and bridling your mount is called.

Yet there is an art to it, and a serious horseman or horsewoman should learn how to do it. Tacking up is an important function preceding every ride and can be simply done if you follow a few basic steps.

Before you begin to tack up, be sure your horse is haltered and tied. Allow enough room so you can work on it from both sides. But before you haul out your saddle and bridle, you should check your grooming job. Be particularly sure that you haven't left any dirt on the horse's back, especially where the saddle fits, or around the girth line where the cinch is tightened. Dirt or dried flakes of sweat can cause galling and sores. The horse's hooves should also be carefully cleaned out, before and after each ride.

Also check your saddle pad or blanket for any burrs, thistles, or other irritating things that might be clinging to it. With everything clean, lay the pad on the horse's back. Place it a few inches farther forward over the withers than where it actually belongs. Then move it back smoothly to its proper place, following the natural rearward lay of the hair. Center the pad so it hangs an equal distance down each side. Now you are ready for the saddle.

There is a lot of difference in weight and bulk between a Western stock saddle and the lighter, simpler English saddle. In fact, the stock saddle is sometimes too heavy for an eager but small horse lover to wrestle up onto a horse's back. The same young rider may be too small to reach up to the mount's ears, which is necessary in order to put on the bridle. If so, the rider should ask for help. He or she shouldn't try to fling the saddle up onto the horse and perhaps spook it with flying straps and banging stirrups.

But, assuming that you are strong enough and tall enough to tack up your horse, get your saddle from its storage rack and proceed. Before you pick it up off the rack, however, lay anything up over the seat that normally hangs down on the right side of the saddle—like the stirrup, cinch, and saddle strings. Get them up and out of the way. On the Western stock saddle, you can hook the right stirrup over the horn.

Pick your saddle up from the left side. Carry it by the pommel or horn with your left hand, while your right hand grips the cantle or perhaps the rear skirt of the stock saddle.

Carrying the saddle about waist high, approach the horse on the near, or left, side, but enough in front so your mount can see you clearly and be prepared for what's to come. In fact, you might talk to it a bit as you come. Some horses do not like the idea of being saddled up, and a little cajoling may help set a calm mood.

Once beside the horse, lift and swing the saddle up onto its back. Do so rhythmically and gently, and set it down easily onto the pad. Handling the English saddle is simpler than the heavy stock saddle, but in either case the chore is quickly finished.

Gripping pommel and cantle, shake the saddle down a little. Feel it settle properly into place. Most saddles adapt to a particular horse's back, and you can tell easily when the saddle lies right.

Now go around to the off, or right, side. Check the blanket or pad to see that it's squared off with equal margins around the skirt. From the right side now reach

Lift the saddle and lay it gently over the pad.

up and drop the cinch, the stirrup, and straps. Be sure all straps are untwisted, and nothing is out of place or has been caught or folded under the saddle.

Return to the near side and place the stirrup in the saddle's seat, so that you will be free to work on the cinch ring. Reach under and get hold of the cinch or girth, and bring it up around the horse's girth line. Keep it far enough behind your mount's elbows so as not to interfere with front-leg action.

Tighten the cinch.

Now the Western rider will run the cinch strap, or
latigo, through the cinch ring and tighten it. The cinch
used to be tied to whatever tension the rider wanted by
using a cinch hitch or knot. Now most cinch rings are

built like a buckle, and the cinch is secured very much like a common tongued belt buckle. The English rider simply secures the girth to the two buckles under the saddle skirt.

Don't cinch up too tight. You needn't try to squeeze the breath out of the horse. Tighten the cinch snugly, but leave enough room between it and the horse's side so you can insert two fingers.

Walk your horse around and check the cinch again before you mount, for many a cinch-wise horse swells up and holds its breath while you are tightening the strap. But a few minutes later, after it relaxes and lets out its breath, you can put the proper tension on the cinch. Lower the stirrup, and the saddling is finished.

If you are a Western rider, you may also use a flank, or back cinch, which should be tightened only to within a couple of inches of the horse's belly. However, flank cinches are used normally only during extra strenuous riding, such as roping, where the saddle is under heavy strain and the double cinches are needed to keep it in place. Remember always to fasten it last when saddling, and unfasten it first when unsaddling.

Next comes the bridling. Regardless of the type of bridle you use—and there are numerous styles and types —the procedure for putting it on is fundamentally the same. Your horse is still in its halter as you approach on the near side with the bridle. Carry the bridle in the crook of your arm, as you reach up and unbuckle the halter. Let the halter drop below the horse's nose, and move it back on its neck and rebuckle it. Thus, your mount remains tethered while you do the actual bridling.

You may put the reins up over its head so they rest on the neck, or you can drape the reins over your own shoulder while you maneuver the bridle into place. Just be sure the reins are up and out of your way, not dangling to the ground where your horse can step on them.

As always when you are dealing with a horse, be positive in your actions. If it senses uncertainty on your part, it may give you a bad time. Move slowly and deliberately. Let the horse know you are boss, but assert yourself firmly rather than roughly.

Hold the top of the headstall, with your right hand resting on your horse's forehead between the ears. Support the bit in your left hand. On a Western bit, use your little finger to hold the curb strap or chain back out of the way, so it won't also go into your horse's mouth. Now, with your right hand, lift the headstall up its face toward its ears, thus drawing the bit near its lips.

Lift the bit toward its mouth.

Many horses will automatically open up when they see the bit coming toward their mouth. However, some will pretend it isn't there or, worse, try to dodge it. Here, again, be firm. If it doesn't accept the bit readily, wiggle a finger in its mouth on the side at the toothless bar area, and the horse should open up and take it. Keep pulling up on the headstall, bringing the bit back in its mouth and atop its tongue. Once the bit is in place, bend your mount's ears forward and slip the crownpiece of the headstall over them. Pull its forelock out from under the browband.

If the bridle has a throatlatch, check to see that it isn't tight against the windpipe. Loosen it enough to slip three fingers under it. Also see that you can slip a finger easily under the curb chain. Adjust the cheek pieces so the bit is drawn up into the mouth just enough to put a small, comfortable wrinkle at the corners.

Bridling is not always a simple procedure, but practice helps. Now, as you remove the halter and look everything over for a final time, you are ready to mount.

Mounting up is just as much a gentle art as any other part of horsemanship. It is graceful and effective when done properly. When done improperly, it not only makes a clumsy sight, it disturbs your horse, sometimes enough so that it will try and unseat you.

As with all phases of horsemanship, let your horse know what you are about to do. Approach it at about the shoulder from the left side. All work around your horse, in fact, is done from this near side. Talk to it as you stroke it.

You may face its side or, as is probably more frequently done, face rearward. Reach up near the mane and collect the reins in your left hand. Have just enough tension on them to make contact with your horse's mouth, so it is "on the bit" and in check. With reins still in hand, take hold of the horse's mane just ahead of the withers.

Now, with your right hand, turn the stirrup toward you so that when you swing up and around, the stirrup

Foot in stirrup and left hand grasping mane,
you are prepared to swing up into the saddle.

leather will lie flat against the saddle. Lift your left foot and slip it into the stirrup to the ball of your foot.

On a stock saddle you may now reach either for the horn or for the cantle with your right hand. It's always the cantle on an English saddle, for there is no horn to grasp. You now have four good points of contact— hand on mane, hand on cantle, ball of left foot in stirrup, and right foot on the ground.

Next, get into your rhythm and pull up with both

Swing your right leg clear of the horse's rump.

Settle gently into the seat.

hands as you spring off the ground with your right foot. Keep your back straight as you rise up into the stirrup. Now as you rotate forward, lift your right leg and swing it over your horse's rump. Be careful not to brush the horse with your toe or kick it. Let your leg continue down the offside toward the stirrup. Don't thump down into the saddle, but lower yourself gently onto the seat, and then calmly find the stirrup with your right foot.

The whole operation should be done in smoothly

flowing style. Always be sure that you are in contact, that is, have control of your horse. Even if it takes a step or two forward—a common reaction when you are mounting—the movement will only serve to aid your upward swing and rotation into the saddle.

If your horse tends to shy its rear end away from you while you are mounting, pull on the right rein, which will twist its head to the right and bring its rear toward you where it belongs. Use opposite reining if it tries to move away from you at the neck end.

You dismount in pretty much the reverse order, except for a few important differences. First, if you are inclined to ride with your feet deep in the stirrups, be sure that your left foot is well out to the toes in the stirrup. Then if anything goes wrong during dismounting, you won't get hung up.

Again, holding the reins in your left hand and grabbing a piece of mane or neck, slip your right foot from its stirrup, and swing your right leg back over the horse's rump. Be sure to clear it, for again a brush or kick could be a false signal for your horse to move or even leap ahead. And this moment is a poor time for any movement.

Swing your right foot around and bring it to rest next to your left foot, which is still in its stirrup. Now support yourself in that position with one hand on the neck and the other on the seat or the cantle. With your weight thus on your arms, remove your left foot from the stirrup. At this point most English riders push slightly away from the horse and simply slide down, both feet touching the ground together. The Western rider, however, continues to swing the right leg to the ground first, then takes the left foot out of the stirrup.

There are, indeed, various versions of mounting and dismounting, but any approved method follows pretty much these basic steps. Practice them and master them, and add to your skill as a rider.

chapter seven

RIDE WESTERN

As a young Western rider you've probably had visions of getting all dolled up in hand-stitched boots, buckskin chaps, and a fancy, embroidered Western shirt, topped off with a ten-gallon hat. Thus "turned out," you vault into the saddle of an impatient red roan and gallop off through the mesquite as jackrabbits flee before you.

This dream may be what got you interested in horses to begin with. Surely, riding with such carefree abandon around the countryside is one of the many delights of horsemanship.

But, in order to get the most pleasure with the greatest safety from any kind of riding, you should first learn the horse's basic gaits and be able to perform them with skill and style. The best place to start is not out on the long trail, but in an enclosed area where you can control the action and where your horse is less inclined to take the bit in its teeth and head for the tall timber.

The primary gait of any horse is the ordinary walk, during which three hooves are usually in ground contact while the fourth moves. It is a most simple gait, indeed, but when done under proper bridle control and riding aids, it becomes a smooth stride, not a lazy shuffle. When speeded up, the walk shifts to a jog, or what English riders would call a slow trot. In a jog, the diagonal legs—that is, left front and right hind, or right front and left hind—move together in the same direction. The jog is the bounciest of the Western gaits.

The third, and still faster gait, is the lope. The lope is similar to what the English rider refers to as a canter. Each actually is a slow gallop. The fourth and fastest riding gait is the thundering full gallop, common to both Western and English riding, but used sparingly.

While you practice the different gaits, you will learn the fundamentals of reining and how to use other aids to start, stop, and guide your horse. You get acquainted

Basic riding can best be learned
in an enclosed area.

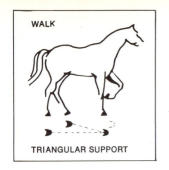

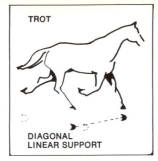

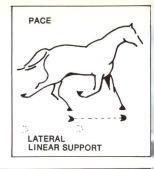

the gaits of horses

with it too. You learn to match the rhythm of your moves with your mount's. You quickly discover that it has feelings the same as yours. If you are calm and gentle with it, the horse will respond favorably. If you treat it harshly, make unfair demands, and use rough techniques, it will become distrustful, skittish, and difficult to handle.

After you have gained a lot of riding skill and built a friendly, working relationship between you and your horse, you may want to enter different kinds of competition, including both riding and showing.

Horse shows of all sizes and varieties are run year around in one place or another. Usually you can locate one within easy trailering distance from your home. Also, you will find events geared to all age ranges and various degrees of skill. Any of them will give you the chance to enjoy the company of others who share similar interests, to see all kinds of horses and tack, and to compete for fun and trophies.

Most important of all, when you enter competition, you make the effort to look your best and work hard with your horse to do its best, the only way to become a really competent horseman or horsewoman.

In some shows you may enter your horse in any number of riding events—Western, English, or both. There are general similarities in the two styles of riding, but also basic differences that need to be considered separately.

In riding Western style, you learn to assume a straight-up, balanced stock-seat position in the saddle as opposed to the more forward, raised hunt-seat position used in English riding. In the stock seat you generally ride deep in the saddle, while English riders are usually suspended just above the seat.

Once you have settled into your Western saddle, adjust the reins in your left hand so that you have gentle contact with your horse's mouth. Although riding styles differ in various parts of the country, the most common method for holding split reins is to run them in the top and out the bottom of your loosely closed left fist. With your thumb upward hold the reins directly over or slightly ahead of the saddle horn. Rest your right hand casually on your right thigh.

If you use the popular California-style, braided raw-

The usual Western method for holding split reins.

hide reins, you will have a long, third section called a "romal" attached. In this case, you run the reins from the bottom of your hand upward and out the top. Drape the romal to the off side and hold it loosely in the right hand resting on your thigh.

Sit erectly but not stiffly in the saddle. Keep some flexibility in your ankles, knees, and in the small of your back so you are able to move in rhythm with your horse. Keep your shoulders square. In your upright position, your legs and stirrups are directly under your body. Your head, hips, and heels form a straight vertical line.

Have the balls of your feet in solid contact with the inside of the stirrups. Point your heels down. Your heels should always be lower in the stirrups than your toes. This position helps put your weight down your legs and increases the security of your seat. Have your elbows in close to your body, not angled out. Do not swing them out wide as is sometimes shown in Western movies.

The inside of your thighs, knees, and upper calves lie against the seat or fenders of your saddle. By sitting well down in the saddle, use them to support some of your weight and absorb the shocks of a bouncing ride. These pressures on the sides of your saddle will help keep you a little forward in the seat, not sitting back on your tailbone.

Sit in the saddle with head up, heels down,
and back straight, but not rigid.

Keep your head up and your eyes looking straight between the ears of your horse. If you must glance around at all, do so with eye movements, not by turning your head. Look comfortable and confident. Be in balance with your horse, and the rest will come easily.

Sitting properly in the saddle, you are ready to move. In order to communicate your wishes to your horse, you must use your hands, legs, body, and voice. Use them as lightly as you can and still get the desired response from your horse. You may have other aids available, such as spurs, a quirt (whip), or the end of the romal. But the use of these artificial aids should be avoided if possible. You are a much better horse rider if you can control your mount with natural cues.

Perhaps you are in the arena ready to perform a bit of equitation in front of a judge. To urge your horse into a walk, simply ease off a little on the reins, shift your weight slightly forward, and squeeze gently with your legs. Any well-trained horse will get the message immediately and move ahead. Once it is into the walk, release the leg pressure, and take the bit up slightly, keeping mouth contact. Be careful not to put so much tension on the reins that your horse will pull to a stop. Western horses are neck reined. So if you want to turn right, simply move your hand to the right. This movement lays the left rein softly against the left side of your horse's neck. At the same time gently press your left leg against its side. Your horse will move away from any applied pressures and make a right turn. Release both pressures as soon as it has turned as far as you want it to. Otherwise, it will continue turning a full circle or more.

Your horse must be able to depend upon you. So be careful that you don't give it false or mixed-up signals. Don't rein it for a right turn and give it knee or heel pressure for a left turn. If you confuse your mount by urging it forward with a hard kick of your heels, and at the same time jerk back on the reins, it is apt to jump in confusion and unseat you. The least that will happen is that your horse soon will decide that it cannot trust your signals, and your riding will suffer greatly for it.

At all times communicate to your horse with body language. When you pull back on the reins to stop it, also settle yourself back in the saddle. If you turn left, lean your weight left. When urging your horse ahead, lean slightly forward to stay in balance as it accelerates. Otherwise, you may be left behind and unable to co-ordinate with its moves.

Use your voice too. A quiet cluck, a soft "whoah," or a word or two it has learned to understand may be all you need to start, stop, or alter the action of your horse.

Normally, however, if you are changing from a walk to a jog, use your leg pressure, rein aids, plus a slight forward shift of balance. You may add a soft cluck or two with your tongue. The Western jog actually is a little slower and smoother than the English-style trot, and in it you maintain your full upright position, never leaning forward.

The jog is a bouncing gait. You may have trouble sitting down in your saddle when your horse is jogging, but you should do so when you are riding stock seat. By using your thigh, knee, and leg pressures as shock absorbers, you will soon master the skill. Once you get into natural rhythm with your horse, you will have no difficulty.

A prime concern in Western equitation riding, with its slow gaits, is to keep your horse properly gathered in, or collected. Be sure you are in full control and that your horse is prepared before you make a move. Square yourself in the saddle, and put just enough tension on the reins to place your horse on the bit and draw its head in a little. This pressure perks it up in anticipation of the cue to come.

Having done so, urge him to speed up from a jog to a lope, or slow gallop. During a lope, you need to be concerned with the correct lead. The lead is the sequence in which your horse's forefeet reach out and strike the ground while in a lope, a canter, or indeed, during a full-out gallop. If its left front hoof strikes the ground farther forward than the right, it is on a left lead. If its right foreleg is the one reaching farther out, it is on a right lead.

When riding a straight course, the lead your horse is on doesn't matter. It will pick whichever one is most comfortable. However, when riding a circular path, counterclockwise, it should be on a left lead; when clockwise, it should be on a right lead. In this way your horse is in better balance for turning at a lope, and the ride is easier on you.

Here, again, to set the correct lead gather your horse in momentarily just before urging it into a lope, so it will be ready to heed your signals. If you are jogging in a counterclockwise direction, you collect it with your reins. Then give it firm pressure or a light kick with your right leg or foot. Just as your horse is about to break stride and go into a lope, rein its head a little to the right, or toward the outside rail. Your weight should be solid in the saddle, and with these actions it will be natural for your horse to reach out with its left or inside foreleg. Its left hind leg will also be ahead of the right. Thus you will have put it on a left lead. Later, if you should turn and go clockwise, you need only reverse the procedure and put it on the right lead.

Don't bend over or look down to see if your horse is on the correct lead. That's a sure way to lose points with the judge. Keep your head up and eyes straight ahead. With practice, you can feel your horse's movements beneath you, and by its balanced rhythm tell whether it is on the proper lead.

(Pacing, a fifth gait, is used primarily for showy Saddlebred horses and in harness racing.)

Once you and your horse have a working partnership, your most subtle and gentle signals will rate a quick response. As you become more and more at home in the stock saddle, try some simple maneuvers such as circles, figure eights, and serpentines. Start with wide circles and tighten them up as you learn to use your aids properly and as your horse learns to respond quickly and easily to them.

While performing figure eights at a jog there's an especially good opportunity in the middle of the eight to practice stops. Stopping, of course, is not a matter of just hauling back on the bit. You collect your horse subtly. Then, when you judge by the rhythm of the gait that it can stop without breaking awkwardly into the middle of a stride, shift your body weight a little to the rear. At the same time, give a soft "whoah," and pull lightly on the reins. Always use the reins lightly, because if you have to pull on the bit so hard that your horse's mouth comes open, you've made a bad stop. Remember always to warn it that you want it to stop. A trained horse will heed your "whoah" and begin to stop before you've even touched the reins. When your mount comes to a standstill and levels off, you should be upright and firm in your saddle, the basic seat.

Doing serpentines across a paddock or arena allows

you to rein left and right, and also to change gaits if you wish. In all riding practices remember to keep switching what you are doing. Don't walk too long, or jog back and forth endlessly, or lope a great deal on one lead. Both you and your horse can become bored with such sameness. And by all means try more difficult maneuvers as you go along.

Early in your riding career you should discipline yourself at slow-paced gaits in order to establish a proper basic seat and to "become one" with your horse. Yet surely your riding ambitions will not stop there. You will begin to think of taking carefree trail rides through uncertain terrain. Your long-range plans may even include some of the more action-packed events of western riding.

You may want to enter a trail-horse event in which you guide your horse around, through, and over obstacles such as wooden bridges, a tangle of logs, gates, and water hazards. A horse is inclined to be skittish of anything in its path or around it. In trail-horse competition your horse must ignore these instincts and trust you. Perhaps one of the tests may be to determine how well you can urge your horse into a trailer. Often it is one of the more difficult tests.

You may want to enter the reining competition, with

Carefree trail riding is a major joy of horsemanship.

its turning, pivoting, stopping, and backing. One of the most interesting parts of a reining contest is the fast rundown and sliding stop. Using as much of the arena as you can, you urge your horse into a gallop. Pick out a spot some distance ahead where you will stop, or "set him down." Keep that spot in your vision, for if you don't plan ahead you may come to an uncertain and sloppy stop.

Stay well down into your saddle. With your head up and eyes ahead, keep contact with the bit. When you reach your spot, don't make any abrupt moves, but let your weight shift slightly backward on the seat. Flex your knees just enough to take some of the weight off the stirrups. At the same time ease back gently on the reins. From your shift of balance, your horse will catch the cue of what is expected. As soon as it feels the bit, it will drop its haunches, stiffen out its front legs, and come to a dusty square stop. When done properly, a running stop is one of the highlights of good horse-manship.

You may or may not have ambitions for more strenuous types of riding seen at some horse shows and at rodeos. Such things as cow cutting, steer roping, and barrel racing are as much a part of Western riding as are the more gentle pursuits of walking, jogging, and loping.

In addition to riding competition, you may want to show your horse at halter. For this event, you use no saddle or bridle, only your barebacked horse in a halter, with you on the ground holding onto the lead rope. Primarily you will need a horse that is put together correctly, for its conformation is of major concern to the judge.

Barrel racing is competitive fun on horseback.

Before entering the ring, however, you must work hard to spiff up your horse, from polished hooves to shaved muzzle. Wash it, comb it, clip and brush it. Talk to it, pet it. Make it shine and feel good. And, don't forget, you, too, must dress up for the occasion. It's all part of winning.

Once in the ring, stand your horse squarely on all four feet. The stance varies according to breed, with some horses stretching their hind legs farther back than others. Hold the lead strap in such a way that your horse will keep its head up and ears alert.

The judge looks it over from all angles. At his request you walk or trot your horse across the arena as you walk or trot alongside. The judge wants to see if your horse moves well and is sound. Your own appearance and your ability to work with your horse are bound to affect his decision. So make the overall impression a good one.

Establish your foundation of horsemanship properly in order to be ready for anything you may want to do while astride your mount or while showing it in the arena. In that way you can insure a contented horse and a happy rider.

chapter eight

RIDE ENGLISH

When riding the English saddle, you do many things the same way as when riding Western stock seat. You use the necessary leg aids and body language. You ride substantially upright over your stirrups, making minor shifts in your center of gravity to keep in balance with your horse. You ride with head up and heels down.

The first of the English gaits is the standard walk. Then comes the trot, in which diagonal front and rear hooves move in the same direction, but at a bit more sprightly rate than the Western jog. The third gait is the canter, or slow gallop, which is similar to but also a little faster than the Western lope. The fourth gait is the full gallop.

Despite overall similarities in gaits, there are some basic differences in English and Western riding. English riding is usually a more sensitive and formal style of riding than the more rugged, working, ranch-hand type of stock-seat horsemanship.

Actually there are two main styles of riding English. One is called the "flat saddle seat," the other the "for-

111

ward hunt seat." The saddle seat (sometimes called the park seat) rider uses a type of flat saddle that has a deeply cut-back pommel so as not to interfere with the action of the horse's high arching neck. This saddle also has a low cantle, thin padding on the side panels, and stirrups that are set long. The idea behind the low-profile saddle is to make it as unnoticeable as possible in order to display the horse better.

The horse used mainly for saddle-seat riding is the high-headed, high-stepping, high-tailed "peacock" of the horse world. The horse is called the American Saddlebred, an American Saddle Horse, or simply a Saddler. The high-stepper is related to the handsome Tennessee Walking Horse, which has a spirited, broken gait called a "singlefoot" or "rack." Dressage is an example of gaited riding wherein a horse is trained to make the best use of strength, agility, and willingness to perform.

Saddle-seat riding styles began more than a century ago when Southern plantation owners gaited their horses to move with an air of exaggerated showmanship, with prancing hooves and proud head held high. Despite the spirited nature of the gaits—and there are five different ones to choose from—the horse's back remains level with little bounce, producing an easy ride.

In saddle-seat riding sit back toward the low cantle

112

Dressage is a formalized English riding style
that develops a horse's strength, agility, and obedience.

in order to remain well clear of the upraised neck and
to keep the balance centered on your mount's back.
Often you will use a full bridle with a double set of
reins. Tension on the snaffle tends to keep your horse's
head up, while the curb bit tucks its chin in, giving it
that regal, erect look.

However, other than for parade or show-ring purposes, Saddlebred horses and saddle-seat riding actually make up a small segment of English riding activity today. Most English pleasure riding is done with a hunt seat, or forward seat. In the hunt seat your balance is closer to your horse's withers. Thus, your horse is better able to support your weight on its forelegs, while its muscular hind quarters are left free to perform their primary job of propulsion.

Most horses are perfectly capable of being ridden either stock seat or hunt seat. But, being a little less burdened with weight, hunter-type horses are schooled to move at a little quicker pace than Western pleasure horses. The hunter walks a little faster, using a smart trot instead of a slow jog. It canters instead of lopes. The English walk and canter are ridden basically the same way as the Western walk and lope. However, the trot requires a minor change in riding technique. In the stock-saddle jog you learn to ride with the slight bounce while sitting deep in the saddle. But the hunt-seat trot, being faster, generates more bounce. To keep in rhythm with your horse and to help propel him forward, you must learn to post.

In English riding you use two hands on the reins. One rein is in each hand and held along the sides of the horse's neck forward of the withers. Instead of neck reining, as with the stock horse, you direct rein, that is, you pull on one rein while easing off an equal amount of pressure on the other. Pull right to turn right, left to turn left. You ease the reins forward equally and use leg signals to move ahead. When you want to stop, put rearward tension on the reins.

In the hunt seat you also shorten the stirrups enough so you can rise smoothly off the seat by the simple flexing of your ankles, knees, and upper legs.

To post, you simply anticipate your horse's bounce,

Sitting the hunt seat.

use a little of its force, plus your leg muscles, to help you rise slightly forward and up off the seat. Having thus lifted your rear end out of the saddle for a moment, you stay there through one stride, then ease back down in the saddle.

Posting is strictly a matter of getting in tempo with your horse and maintaining it during the trot. Your horse should do most of the work. If you find yourself pushing up from your stirrups, you're not posting properly. You must use your leg and thigh muscles. And if you get out of cadence with your horse's movements—going down when it is coming up—you will take a heavier thumping than if you had just remained in the saddle. When you are posting correctly, there will be scarcely any open space between you and the saddle, and there will be no perceptible jarring action in rising from or returning to the seat.

Just as the correct lead is necessary while loping or cantering on a curved course, so you should take care to post on the correct diagonal on a curved course.

Unlike cantering, where both hooves on one side usually move together, diagonal hooves move together in trotting. The near (left) foreleg and off (right) hind leg move forward at the same time, while the other two diagonal hooves move rearward.

If you are trotting around the arena clockwise, you rise in the saddle as the left forefoot reaches out forward. It is easy to remember to rise up when the forefoot nearest the outside rail extends forward. You return to the saddle during the next stride, and post again as the cycle repeats.

Since you should always keep your head up and eyes looking forward, a mere glance at your horse's shoulders will tell you which leg is moving out front and you can adjust your posting accordingly. An expert rider can tell the correct diagonal by feeling the movement beneath him. If you find you are on the wrong diagonal, simply sit out one stride and get in tempo with the correct diagonal.

So, for straight park-trail riding, and for most of the competitive events in English-riding horse shows, the hunt seat is the all-around favorite. Also use the hunt seat for simply hacking around in the country where you can forget some of the formalities of dress, but should not get sloppy about your riding techniques. However, until you have practiced enough to be competent and confident in the saddle, you should avoid trying your hand at one of the most exciting and demanding events of hunt-seat riding—jumping.

Of course, you do not have to be an expert rider in

a well-executed jump

order to try your hand at jumping logs or other low obstacles. After all, if you learn your techniques carefully, go slowly, and know how to work with your horse, you should have no great problems with taking a few small, leisurely jumps during your ride.

In horse shows, hunting courses are set up to stimulate the classic cross-country style of riding to the hounds and chasing the fox. The hunter must be well-disciplined to maneuver and stand so you can open and close gates while still in the saddle. It must be trained to sidestep simulated bramble thickets, go through water, and contend with potential hazards of that nature. Your horse is required to jump over ditches, low fences, or moderate-sized hedges. The obstacles that a hunter is asked to negotiate are not as high or as complicated as those used for the open jumpers. Generally, however, the training of the two horses is similar.

The whole idea behind jumping is to allow your horse freedom by always remaining in balance with its movements. After all, its muscles and spring are what will get you over the hurdle, and the less interference you give it the better. So, in jumping, your job is to be as light and balanced as you can in the saddle, while still lending a little aid and direction to your horse's efforts.

One of your best aids is confidence. If you have learned to walk, trot, and canter, learned leads and diagonals, and sit a good solid seat, your horse will be the first to know. It will treat you accordingly with respect. If you lack confidence, your horse will know that, too. And you shouldn't be trying to jump.

Start slowly when you begin jumping. Before actually taking any jumps, you should spend time warming up your horse. Ride it around awhile, walking, trotting, and cantering.

Many beginning jumpers prefer a forward seat with padded knee rolls. They can save you from a spill or two. Above all, have good hands, which means light hands. To jab your horse's mouth, or to rely on your reins to keep you in the saddle will surely ruin any efforts at the fences.

At the beginning you should guide your horse over a few low obstacles such as rails laid across the path. Let it merely trot over them while you post gently. Do so many times, so that it can establish a rhythm and cadence while going over the rails.

Before you move to a little higher barrier of about a foot, watch another experienced rider. See how this rider moves out at a canter, gathering in his mount a little and timing, or rating, the canter during the last few yards, so the horse will go over the obstacle without breaking stride. Watch him use his reins to keep the horse on course, loosely enough so as not to upset his mount's stride or freedom of movement.

Notice the horse's actions as its head and neck move up and forward, and then downward as it goes over the the low barrier. If you realize that this graceful flexibility of its neck is your mount's prime means of balance over the jump, you will understand why you should not interfere with it. As the fences get higher, this element of giving the horse freedom increases in importance.

Now your turn comes. As you approach the fence, you lean slightly forward out of the saddle and put your weight well out ahead. You have assumed the half-seat position. Keep your feet firmly in the stirrups, heels down. Lay your legs against your horse's side, with leg and thigh muscles tight and secure. You must learn to maintain this balanced position at all times while going over the fence. The proper amount of lean puts your weight over your horse's shoulders and leaves its hindquarters free to propel both you and it over the fence. Without this balance, you will be in a precarious position and the recovery after landing will be very difficult.

During the jump you lower your hands and reins to each side of your horse's neck, so your forearms and reins make a straight line to the bit. In this manner you will have full control upon landing. But stay off the bit while your horse goes over the barrier. There is no way you can help lift it over with your reins. Instead, you can easily spoil the jump by hauling back and ruining its balance.

To land properly, absorb the action by forcing your weight down your legs to your heels. Now sink softly back into your saddle and keep your course in mind, eyes always looking ahead.

Since the course laid out in the arena may zigzag and have short approaches between barriers, you must help your horse. You must show it where to go by skillful use of the reins. You must be able to collect your mount in properly, judge the distance to the fence, control the gait, and give it its head at the exact time and distance it needs to build up the right momentum to get over the fence.

On a well-executed jump, you will delight in the feel of the hindquarters clearing the crossrail without the faulting sound of a hoof thumping on wood.

As you become more expert, and the courses more difficult, new problems occur. If all things are not right, your horse may become confused and shy from the barrier. You must circle and try again, and again, if necessary. If you let it get away with balking or shying, you will lose control and find that your mount has developed a bad habit that will be hard to break.

For most English riders the most exhilarating experience is taking a jump cleanly, for hours of daily work are needed before you truly become one with your horse.

On the other hand, many enthusiastic horse lovers

will find similar thrills showing at halter, riding a mountain trail, or hacking along a bridle path with a bunch of friends.

Indeed, just being around horses, working with them, caring for them, riding them, liking them—that is what horsemanship is all about.

The thrill of jumping is a peak reward
of good horsemanship.

Aged—a horse nine or more years old.

Aids—devices such as the voice, hands, legs, spurs, used by the rider to cue a horse.

Bars—gaps in the teeth of horse's lower jaw where the bit rests.

Billets—straps that secure the cinch or girth.

Bit—the mouthpiece of a bridle.

Box stall—a square-shaped, roomy stall.

Breed—an animal strain that reproduces the characteristics by which it is recognized.

Bridle—a head-fitting leather assembly consisting of a headstall, to which the reins and bit are attached.

Canter—a three-beat gait, slow gallop or a fast lope.

Cantle—the curved, upthrust rear end of a saddle.

Cavesson—the noseband of an English bridle.

Center-fire rig—a Western saddle with a single-centered cinch.

Cinch—the girth strap that holds a western saddle in place.

Colt—a male horse under the age of four years.

Conformation—the way a horse's physical parts are put together.

Crossbred—offspring of parents of different horse breeds.

Curb—a bit with a low part and slightly curved shanks used primarily in Western tack.

Direct rein—English style of reining in which the rider turns a horse right by pulling on the corresponding right rein, and vice versa.

Dressage—a system of training aimed to fully develop a horse's capabilities.

Equitation—a style of riding in general, or a horse class in which the rider is judged more than the horse itself.

Farrier—a horseshoer.

Filly—a female horse under the age of four years.

Forward seat—English style of riding in which the rider keeps his weight up over the horse's withers. In jumping, this is known as the hunt seat.

Gait—one of a horse's paces, such as walk, trot, canter, etc.

Gallop—a fast canter.

Gelding—a castrated stallion.

Girth—the strap that holds an English saddle in place. Similar to a Western cinch.

Grade—a horse or pony of mixed parentage.

Hackamore—a bitless bridle.

Hand—a four-inch unit by which a horse's height is measured.

Headstall—see bridle.

Horn—the projection from a Western saddle pommel used to secure a lariat during stock work.

Hunt seat—see forward seat.

Irons—a term used for English stirrups.

Leathers—straps that attach the stirrups to an English saddle.

Lope—a slow canter.

Longeing (or lunging)—to exercise a horse in circles on the end of a longe line.

Mare—a female horse over the age of four years.

Near side—the left side of a horse.

Neck rein—Western style of reining in which the rider turns a horse right or left by applying pressure on the opposite rein against the horse's neck.

Off side—the right side of a horse.

Pelham—a bit composed of a curb and snaffle.

Pommel—the front part of a saddle.

Pony—any horse fewer than fourteen hands, two inches high (58 inches).

Post—to rise and fall in the saddle in rhythm with a horse's trot gait.

Saddle horse—a breed of high-stepping, high-headed horses (also Saddler).

Saddle seat—a formal style of English riding in which the rider sits back in the saddle so as to display the high-headed, high-stepping action of the horse.

Snaffle—a simple bit jointed in the middle, used primarily in English riding.

Sound—a horse in good condition and health.

Stallion—an adult male horse that has not been castrated.

Stock-seat equitation—a style of riding the Western saddle.

Tack—any equipment used on a horse, such as halter, bridle, saddle, etc.

Trot—a two-beat gait.

126

index

* indicates illustration